WHEN I WAS FURTHEST FROM WATER

First edition. First printing, 2018
ISBN 978-1-9993065-2-6

WORDS © JOANNA HRUBY 2018
PHOTOGRAPHS © MICHAELA MEADOW 2018
COVER ARTWORK © RIMA STAINES 2018

Litho-printed on 100% recycled paper by CALVERTS
workers co-op in England.

WHEN I WAS FURTHEST FROM WATER is set in
Galliard.

NOTE:
*The photography was shot in the village of Sant Llorenc de
Balàfia, Ibiza, Spain.*

WHEN I WAS FURTHEST FROM WATER

JOANNA HRUBY

WITH PHOTOGRAPHY BY
MICHAELA MEADOW

HEDGESPOKEN PRESS
2018

WHEN I WAS FURTHEST FROM WATER is part of the *Seven Doors in an Unyielding Stone* series.

The titles in the series are:

TWILIGHT – *Jay Griffiths*
BLACK HAT – *Tom Hirons*
WHEN I WAS FURTHEST FROM WATER – *Joanna Hruby*
BULL · POPPY · STAR – *Sylvia V. Linsteadt*
THE FIVE FATHOMS – *Martin Shaw*
NINE PRAISE RIDDLES – *Rima Staines*
SEVEN LITTLE TALES – *Terri Windling*

See WWW.HEDGESPOKENPRESS.COM/SEVEN-DOORS for more about the series.

WHEN I WAS
FURTHEST FROM
WATER

I.

I've always been here,
On an island.
Inside a veil of cicada drone.
With the smell of wild fennel,
And honey-coloured dirt at my feet.
Water was in me at the beginning,
I forgot it aged about seven,
But trouble came –
Made me go hunting
For the source.
I came from water,
It was a long road back.
I'm going back, now.

2.

In this still place I stand,
Juniper, sage and thyme
In my hand.
Speaking now, to
That other girl, who's still back there –
She's in a bedroom in England,
All dark green
Small repeated elephants
And a tall, horrible cupboard.
And although, there on the floor,
She knows I am with her,
Her wailing sails out of the window,
Over the wall,
And to the knarled oak tree
At the end of the field,
Which will soon be covered
by a *Bovis* housing estate.

3.

Font of Balàfia,
For that is your name,
I feel my grandmother near.
She was in the kitchen,
That dull Saturday afternoon
When I swung on the door,
Toes balanced on the doorstop,
And said that
All things felt as empty
As that field
With the oak tree at the end.
I was nine; she understood.
Took me walking on the sea wall,
Fed me words from books,
And sat beside me as I drew.
Yes, *Font of Balàfia,*
My grandmother is here.

4.

I'm at a door, jade green:
So barren,
The long path trudged away from water.
I recall from nine years to eleven,
That endless drought,
When no water is inside you
But you remember the trace –
Tragic.
Sharp words sit there for years,
Like beached shipwrecks.
There was a while when I went to church each
Sunday
With Katherine – we liked the routine, it felt
Strong, disciplined:
I would need that,
To make the walk back
To water.

5.

Elation:
One English autumn,
It arrived within –
The first drone song of cicada
After an interval spanning childhood.
Something moving –
Rumbles from below
In ancient, long-blocked water courses.

The Kingsteignton motorway turn-off:
My mother hands me a PE bag
With newly-embroidered letters
Like a blessing.
A coach rolls in
And I'm terrified.
Through tinted windows
Lies my future –

I look up into it, whilst
Clinging to a knarled oak tree
Behind my eyes.
And there he is,
Whoever he is –
He's looking at the oak tree too.

When I love him into adulthood,
Unrealised,
He will show me back to water.

6.

Forest herbs give way
To the heaviness of air
Surrounding enclosed water.
Now, too, I smell the reek of fish
That filled the boot of my father's car
That summer when my legs were bare,
The earth was moving,
And each day in his chef's whites
He'd play the same album, on loop,
Circling the Penn Inn roundabout.
He was ecstatic.
The music of that island
We remembered:
Calling,
Rising up
In him and his daughter, her
Summer love to bloom and then die
As a new voice got stronger.

7.

A negative space inside –
I spent years tending to it.
Things began
That Thursday lunchtime
When I left the jungle of a
Girls' school classroom,
And sat, sealed
In a toilet cubicle.
You could say
The negative space
Got out of hand – it scared my mother.
She bought books,
Abandoned Western medicine,
And took me to a healer in Ipplepen –
Via *Fermoy's* garden centre.
The negative space scared me too,
But I couldn't turn back.
It was a dry vessel,
Ready –
Ready.
Waiting to be filled.

8.

The cicadas have neatly
Raised their drone one notch.
Perfectly timed –
An orchestrated trance state,
With me within.
It seems right,
To disrobe at the end of a
Much longer journey
Of disrobing.
Fifteen years ago outside the
Hotel Tagomago,
In San Antonio,
We emptied our suitcases on the sand,
And threw away our package holiday:
We wanted rebirth.
So with our stolen bed sheets
And our journals,
We hitch-hiked north –
To get naked.
To drink our dry souls
Wet.

9.

In later years, it was
All about the Waiting.
Someone heard it in my voice one day:
They told me
In the world of Stories,
A man can wander,
Lost in the forest,
For seven years.
I always remembered it.
But years passed and I found the way,
To come back.
My reward –
An outhouse in December
At a strange, ruinous place:
The bejeweled interior of winter hills
And my medicinal forest,
Dripping with rain.

10.

At the threshold of water,
Death lies near –
There is no turning back
When you're almost inside.
A goodbye at Heathrow airport:
I look behind and see
A warm face,
A life about to end.
Ahead I walk,
Through a screen of tears,
To blinding light and X-ray machines.
Somewhere on the way to America,
A new world begins.

Of course you must end worlds
Over, and over, and over again
To find water.

The encounter with water
Is illicit:
Quick, numb and
Shocking.
I crawl into cold, liquid black,
And wash it all away.
Wash away.
A final pit stop
Was the city that,
For three years, had
Covered up my secret.
As I made it out, the car spluttered
And ran out of petrol.
A lame, final war cry.
The water is
Thrilling, and biting cold.
Wash away.

12.

I saw it coming,
Over the course of that final year –
The island
Opened.
It was a forgotten emerald pool
Near San Carles,
With fruit trees beneath;
Where the well-drinkers came.
They said he was no good,
The sitar player,
And they were right.
But he played the music
Of the island's hidden waters,
And by the summer's end,
When he had gone,
I was in.

13.

I've always been here,
On an island.
Inside a veil of cicada drone.
With the smell of wild fennel,
And honey-coloured dirt at my feet.
Water was in me at the beginning,
I forgot it aged about seven,
But it always returns.

HEDGESPOKEN PRESS *publishes*
works of beauty, power and old
magic in the form of the printed
word and image.

To keep up with what we do, please
subscribe to our newsletter at:
WWW.HEDGESPOKENPRESS.COM